TABLE OF CONTENTS (EARLY CHILDHOOD)

Overview..i-vi

Breathe

Belly Breathing.......................................2

Belly Breathing (Lying Down)..................3

Big Happy Breath...................................4

Sunshine Breathing (Seated)..................5

Sunshine Breathing (Standing)...............6

Blowing Out the Candle.........................7

Focus

Listening to the Bell.............................10

Looking at Something..........................11

Covering Your Eyes..............................12

Smile Time..13

Clapping Hands, Quiet Hands..............14

Relax

Sitting Peacefully.................................16

Lying Peacefully...................................17

Shaking Like Spaghetti Noodles...........18

Stretch

Seated Mountain..................................20

Standing Mountain...............................21

Being a Butterfly..................................22

Reach for Your Toes (Seated)...............23

Reach for Your Toes (Standing)............24

Star Stretch (Standing).........................25

Star Stretch (Lying Down)....................26

Seated Moon.......................................27

Standing Moon....................................28

Being a Tree..29

TABLE OF CONTENTS (KINDERGARTEN)

Breathe

Big Happy Breath..................................34

Sun Breathing......................................35

Butterfly Breathing..............................36

Reach for a Star Breath........................37

Tall and Small Breathing......................38

Make a Wish Breath............................39

Focus

Listening to the Bell............................42

Sitting Peacefully................................43

I Am Calm..44

Music Scribble....................................45

Looking at One Thing.........................46

Listening to Counting.........................47

Energy Hands.....................................48

Bee's Buzz..50

Relax

Please Relax (Lying Down)..................52

Please Relax (Seated)..........................54

Shake Like Spaghetti...........................56

Covering Your Eyes.............................57

Stretch

Seated Mountain.................................60

Standing Mountain..............................61

Seated Half Moon...............................62

Standing Half Moon............................63

Twist and Count..................................64

Reach for Your Toes (Seated)..............66

Reach for Your Toes (Standing)...........67

INTRODUCTION

OVERVIEW

This manual supports the effective implementation of the Calm Classroom™ Early Childhood and Kindergarten program which is aligned with State Board of Education goals and guidelines for Social and Emotional Learning.

Calm Classroom™ is a research-based curriculum composed of a series of thirty second to three minute mindfulness-based focusing techniques that elicit the "relaxation response" within both students and teachers. Calm Classroom™ practices are facilitated during classroom transitions throughout the day. These techniques encourage school leaders, faculty and students to develop an introspective and non-judgmental orientation. This leads to the development of greater self-awareness, mental focus, emotional control, and calmness. The Calm Classroom™ Early Childhood and Kindergarten program improves the overall school climate and reduces disciplinary problems and bullying.

The Calm Classroom™ curriculum can be implemented on a school or district wide basis or effectively taught by independent teachers. School-wide trainings include professional development for teachers, administrators, social workers and staff, as well as the development of a long-term assessment and support structure.

The Calm Classroom™ techniques are easy to learn and teach. The Calm Classroom™ curriculum consists of breathing, concentration, relaxation and stretching practices.

INTRODUCTION

CALM CLASSROOM™ A RESEARCHED-BASED CURRICULUM

Calm Classroom™ is an evidence-based curriculum that was originally based on a three year study conducted by Dr. Herbert Benson of Harvard Medical School between 1996 and 1998. Benson measured changes in behavioral and academic outcomes in 1,700 students at Horace Mann Middle School in Los Angeles, California, after exposing them to a classroom curriculum that elicited the relaxation response. The research indicated improvements in both classroom behavior and academic performance. The Calm Classroom™ early childhood and kindergarten curriculum adapts these techniques and implementation protocols that were developed during Dr. Benson's research for the capacities of 2 to 6 year old children.

Since its' inception, the Calm Classroom program has been honed and tested in over 100 public schools that contain early childhood through 8th grade classrooms. Since 2008, more than 2000 teachers and 50,000 students have received Calm Classroom training. Calm Classroom has also been influenced by recent research conducted in the field of developmental cognitive neuroscience. This current brain-based research explores the effects of practicing mindfulness-based concentration protocols which have demonstrated improvements in executive brain functions, memory and emotional resilience. The techniques that elicit the relaxation response and mindfulness are the same.

The following will help clarify the meaning of the terms: mindfulness, relaxation response, executive functions, and emotional resilience.

Relaxation response is defined and measured as a release of chemicals in the body and brain that lowers stress, causes the muscles and organs to slow down, and increases blood flow to the brain. To be physically relaxed and mentally alert is the result of elicitation of the relaxation response. The counterpart to the relaxation response is the fight or flight response which causes increased heart rate and blood pressure, slowed digestive functioning, decreased blood flow to the extremities, and increased release of hormones preparing the body to fight or run.

Mindfulness is characterized by an individual paying full attention to the internal and external sensory, emotional and cognitive experiences that occur each moment. When practicing mindfulness, a non-judgemental orientation is adopted towards whatever is experienced.

Executive function is a set of mental processes that helps connect past experience with present action. People use it to perform activities such as planning, organizing, strategizing, paying attention to and remembering details, and managing time and space. Executive function affects learning, in that it allows us to: make plans, keep track of time and finish work on time, keep track of more than one thing at a time, meaningfully include past knowledge in discussions, evaluate

INTRODUCTION

ideas and reflect on our work, change our minds and make mid-course corrections while thinking, reading, and writing, ask for help or seek more information when we need it, engage in group dynamics, and wait to speak until we are called on.

Emotional resilience refers to the ability of an individual to recover from the effects of a stress provoking situation. This capacity for recovering from stressful situations in which the optimal executive functions of the brain are temporarily inhibited, has been shown to improve through the use of mindfulness-based focusing techniques that elicit the relaxation response.

Detailed academic research regarding the short-term and long-term outcomes of implementing a curriculum that promotes mindfulness and/or the elicitation of the relaxation response, can be viewed at: www.calmclassroom.com/research.

The Best Time to Teach Calm Classroom™

It is suggested that each student practice Calm Classroom™ 3 times each day during full day programing and 2 times during half day sessions. The best time to lead Calm Classroom before, during or after morning circle time and following the most quiet and relaxed activities that the students participate in each day. Teachers can post scheduled times in their classrooms so students know when to expect the practice sessions. Leading Calm Classroom activities can also occur at the ***very last stages*** of returning the students to a calm and focused temperament following disruptive behavioral and emotional outbursts.

Using the Calm Classroom™ CD's

Calm Classroom™ CD's are included with the manual. These demonstrate the proper pacing for each technique. The CD's should be used for training purposes only, in early childhood and Kindergarten classrooms.

Introducing Calm Classroom™

What to Expect
Calm Classroom™ activities may seem new and unusual. The majority of students will immediately relax, focus and enjoy the activities, while a small minority may laugh, make comments, or touch or talk to other students.

Private Introductions
Before introducing the curriculum to the general classroom, have classroom aids meet individually with students who may be disruptive. Lead these students in each new technique so they know what to expect.

INTRODUCTION

General Classroom Introduction
Begin with an age appropriate introduction and interactive discussion about Calm Classroom™. Be prepared with a brief explanation of the breathing, concentration, relaxation and stretching techniques that will be used. Explain that students will learn new ways to stretch and relax the body, control breathing, concentrate the mind and be aware of thoughts and feelings. The calming techniques will help students feel more comfortable when things are upsetting, remain relaxed, solve problems and feel healthier, and feel more energetic during long days at school. Use the following questions to help create your lesson plan for this introduction.

Explore Stress and Anxiety

1. What kinds of things make you feel worried, afraid, angry or nervous? Where do you feel that in your body? Can you describe these feelings?
2. When you notice that you feel afraid, angry or nervous, what do you do to make yourself feel more calm, relaxed and comfortable?

Explore the types of reactions experienced when introduced to new and unusual activities
1. Have you ever experienced a new, unusual activity or situation?
2. What do you remember feeling about the activity or situation?
3. How did you express your discomfort? Example: laughing, talking, fear, etc.

Explore Breathing

Explore breathing and how it changes depending on what we are thinking, feeling or doing.
1. Is your breathing fast or slow when you are afraid, angry or nervous?
2. Is your breathing fast or slow when you are very relaxed and calm?

You can relax your body by breathing slowly and deeply. If you breathe quickly you can energize your body and feel more alert.

Explore Focus

Explore the difference between being mentally focused or distracted.
1. Is it easy to read a book if someone is talking to you? Why not?
2. When I am talking to you do you sometimes think about other things? How does this affect your ability to learn?

Staying focused and relaxed helps you learn more easily. Doing one activity while thinking about something else makes it more difficult to learn.

Explore Relaxation

Explore relaxation and how it makes the mind and body feel.
> 1. What does it feel like when your mind and body feel stressed?
> 2. How does stress affect your mood and relationship with others?

Relaxing the mind and body will improve your mood and make interactions with others pleasant and calm.

Explore Stretching

Explore stretching and how it makes the body feel.
> 1. How does your body feel after you have been sitting at your desk or the computer for a long time? What parts of your body ache or are stiff?
> 2. Is it more difficult to stay focused if your body feels tired, stiff or aches?
> 3. What can you do to help your body feel better?

Stretching the body and exercising will bring more energy to your body and mind, and make you feel better.

CONCLUSION

The benefits of Calm Classroom™ are directly related to the consistency, quantity and quality of the practice. Regularity will produce the most effective results. The most important factor in the success of the Calm Classroom program is the teacher's dedication to utilizing the activities and personally participating with the students in the process. Regularity will produce the most effective results. Calm teachers and students will make possible calm schools and calm communities.

EARLY CHILDHOOD

BREATHE

BREATHE

BELLY BREATHING

Sit with your legs crossed.

Sit up as tall as you can.

Can I see everyone sitting up tall?

Now, put your hands on your belly.

Let's slowly breathe in.

Let's slowly breathe out.

Feel your belly go out and in.

Slowly breathe in again.

Slowly breathe out again.

Feel your belly go out and in.

Now, let's try belly breathing with our eyes closed.

Close your eyes.

Slowly breathe in.

Feel your belly go out.

Slowly breathe out.

Feel your belly go in.

Now, put your hands on your knees.

Slowly open your eyes.

Who felt their belly go out and in?

BELLY BREATHING (LYING DOWN)

Lie down on your back.

Get comfortable.

Now, put your toy on your belly.

Look at the toy on your belly.

Let's slowly breathe in.

Let's slowly breathe out.

Watch your toy go up and down.

Slowly breathe in again.

Slowly breathe out again.

Watch your toy go up and down.

Now, let's try belly breathing with our eyes closed.

Close your eyes.

Slowly breathe in and feel your belly go up.

Slowly breathe out and feel your belly go down.

Now, slowly open your eyes.

Who felt their belly go up and down?

BREATHE

BIG HAPPY BREATH

Sit with your legs crossed.

Put your hands on your knees.

Sit up as tall as you can.

Can I see everyone sitting up tall?

Let's reach our arms out to the sides.

Take a big happy breath in.

Breathe out and give yourself a nice hug.

Reach your arms out to the sides again.

Take a big happy breath in.

Breathe out and give yourself a gentle hug.

Now, let's try this with our eyes closed.

Close your eyes.

Reach your arms out to the sides.

Take a big happy breath in.

Breathe out and give yourself one last hug.

Now, think about all of the nice hugs your gave yourself.

Put your hands on your knees.

Take a big breath in.

Breathe out.

Slowly open your eyes.

SUNSHINE BREATHING (SEATED)

Sit with your legs crossed.

Put your hands on your knees.

Sit up as tall as you can.

Can I see everyone sitting up tall?

Take a big breath in.

Breathe out.

Reach your arms out to the sides and straight up to the sky in the shape of a sun.

Take a big breath in.

Breathe out.

Bring your arms out to the sides and down slowly.

Now, let's try it with our eyes closed.

Close your eyes.

Reach your arms out to the sides and straight up to the sky in the shape of a sun.

Take a big breath in.

Breathe out.

Bring your arms out to the sides and down slowly.

Slowly open your eyes.

BREATHE

SUNSHINE BREATHING (STANDING)

Stand with your feet a little bit apart.

Stand up as tall as you can.

Can I see everyone standing up tall?

Take a big breath in.

Breathe out.

Reach your arms out to the sides and straight up to the sky in the shape of a sun.

Take a big breath in.

Breathe out.

Bring your arms out to the sides and down slowly.

Now, let's try this with our eyes closed.

Close your eyes.

Reach your arms out to the sides and straight up to the sky in the shape of a sun.

Take a big breath in.

Breathe out.

Bring your arms out to the sides and down slowly.

Slowly open your eyes.

BLOWING OUT THE CANDLE

Sit with your legs crossed.

Put your hands on your knees.

Sit up as tall as you can.

Can I see everyone sitting up tall?

Pretend it is your birthday and there is a birthday cake and candle right in front of you!

Take a big breath in.

Slowly blow out your candle and make a wish.

Now, let's close our eyes and try again.

Close your eyes.

Take a big breath in.

Slowly blow out your candle and make another wish.

Slowly open your eyes.

FOCUS

FOCUS

LISTENING TO THE BELL

Sit with your legs crossed.

Put your hands on your knees.

Sit up as tall as you can.

Can I see everyone sitting up tall?

We are going to listen to the sound of a bell.

The bell will sound loud at first and then will get quieter and quieter.

Let's listen to the bell until it stops ringing.

Ready?

[Bell ringing]

Now, let's close our eyes and listen to the bell until it stops ringing.

Close your eyes.

[Bell ringing]

Now, listen to the quiet in the room for five seconds.

5…4…3…2…1.

Take a big breath in.

Breathe out.

Slowly open your eyes.

FOCUS

LOOKING AT SOMETHING

Sit with your legs crossed.

Put your hands on your knees.

Sit up as tall as you can.

Can I see everyone sitting up tall?

Let's practice looking at the object in the middle of the circle. *[Choose object]*

Let's look at it for 5 seconds.

5...4...3...2...1.

Now, let's look at it for 10 seconds.

10...9...8...7...6...5...4...3...2...1.

Now, let's rest our eyes.

Close your eyes and keep them closed for 5 seconds.

5...4...3..2..1.

Breathe in.

Breathe out.

Slowly open your eyes.

FOCUS

COVERING YOUR EYES

Sit with your legs crossed.

Put your hands on your knees.

Sit up as tall as you can.

Can I see everyone sitting up tall?

We are going to practice covering our eyes.

First, let's warm up our hands.

Rub your hands together.

Rub your hands fast!

Rub your hands slow.

Now, stop rubbing and make little cups with your hands.

Cover your eyes with your hands.

Now, close your eyes and let your eyes rest.

Breathe in.

Breathe out.

Now, open your eyes and gently put your hands on your knees.

FOCUS

SMILE TIME

Sit with your legs crossed.

Put your hands on your knees.

Sit up as tall as you can.

Can I see everyone sitting up tall?

Take a big breath in.

Breathe out.

Think of something that makes you happy and makes you smile.

Now, on the count of three, we are all going to make our biggest, brightest smile.

Ready…1…2…3…SMILE!

Look around at everyone's beautiful smiles.

Now, show me all of those beautiful smiles!

Let's keeps smiling for 3 more seconds and then we're going to stop smiling and let our cheeks rest.

3…2…1…Stop!

Breathe in and breathe out.

Now, close your eyes.

Think about the thing that makes you smile.

Breathe in.

Beathe out.

Slowly open your eyes.

FOCUS

CLAPPING HANDS, QUIET HANDS

Sit with your legs crossed.

Put your hands on your knees.

Sit up as tall as you can.

Can I see everyone sitting up tall?

Now, let's clap our hands.

Clap fast.

Clap slow.

Clap fast again!

Now, listen to your hands clapping for 3 seconds.

3...2...1.

Stop clapping and put your quiet hands on your knees.

Close your eyes and listen to the quiet for 3 seconds.

3...2...1.

Breathe in.

Breathe out.

Slowly open your eyes.

RELAX

RELAX

SITTING PEACEFULLY

Sit with your legs crossed.

Put your hands on your knees.

Sit up as tall as you can.

Can I see everyone sitting up tall?

We are going to practice sitting peacefully.

Sitting peacefully means your whole body is quiet and not moving.

Close your eyes.

Your eyes are quiet and peaceful.

Your head is quiet and peaceful.

Your shoulders are quiet and peaceful.

Your hands are quiet and peaceful.

Your belly is quiet and peaceful.

Your knees are quiet and peaceful.

Your feet are quiet and peaceful.

Let's practice sitting peacefully for 10 seconds.

10…9…8…7…6…5…4…3…2…1.

Now, take a big breath in.

Breathe out slowly and peacefully.

Slowly open your eyes.

LYING PEACEFULLY

Lie down on your back.

Get comfortable.

We are going to practice lying peacefully.

Lying peacefully means your whole body is quiet and not moving.

Close your eyes.

Your eyes are quiet and peaceful.

Your head is quiet and peaceful.

Your shoulders are quiet and peaceful.

Your hands are quiet and peaceful.

Your belly is quiet and peaceful.

Your knees are quiet and peaceful.

Your feet are quiet and peaceful.

Let's practice lying peacefully for 10 seconds.

10…9…8…7…6…5…4…3…2…1.

Now, let's take a big breath in.

Breathe out slowly and peacefully.

Slowly open your eyes.

Now, gently sit up and put your hands on your knees.

RELAX

SHAKING LIKE SPAGHETTI NOODLES

Stand with your feet a little bit apart.

Stand up as tall as you can.

Let's shake one arm like a spaghetti noodle!

Shake that arm slowly.

Shake that arm fast!

Now, let's shake both spaghetti arms.

Shake them slowly.

Shake them fast.

Keep your arms shaking and shake one leg.

Put that leg down and shake the other leg!

Now, let's shake both arms and both legs.

Now, freeze!

Shake both spaghetti arms and legs again!

Freeze!

Shake both spaghetti arms and legs one more time.

Keep shaking! Shake faster!

Freeze!

Put your arms by your sides and stand very still.

Take a big breath in.

Breathe out slowly.

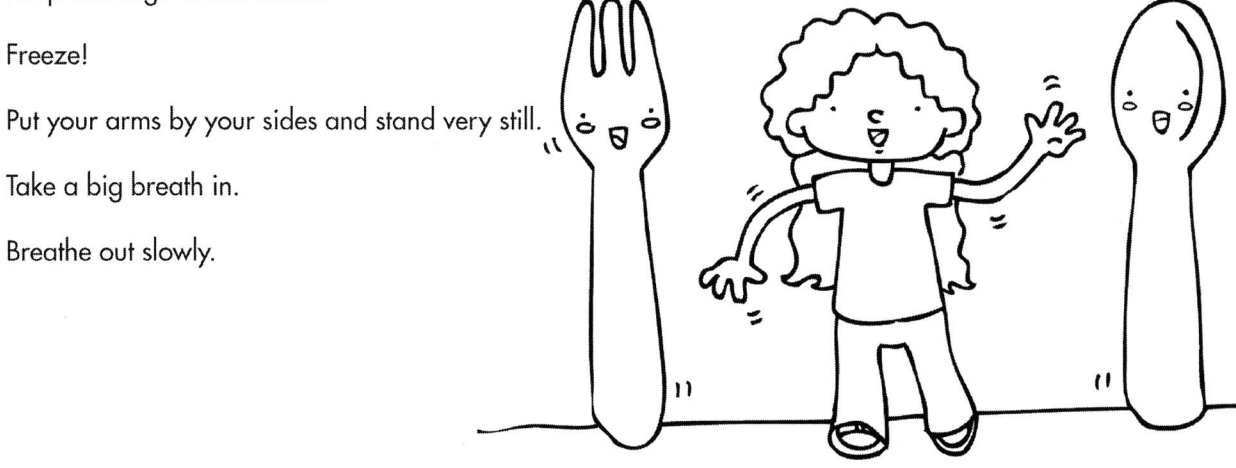

STRETCH

STRETCH

SEATED MOUNTAIN

Sit with your legs crossed.

Put your hands on your knees.

Sit up tall like a mountain.

Can I see everyone sitting up tall?

Reach your arms up to the sky.

Wiggle your fingers.

Make a point with your hands like a tall and pointy mountain.

Reach higher through the clouds and into the sky.

Close your eyes.

Reach even higher for five more seconds.

5…4…3…2…1.

Take a big breath in.

Breathe out and bring your arms down slowly.

Put your hands on your knees.

Slowly open your eyes.

STANDING MOUNTAIN

Stand with your feet a little bit apart.

Stand up tall like a mountain.

Can I see everyone standing up tall?

Reach your arms up to the sky.

Wiggle your fingers.

Make a point with your hands like a tall and pointy mountain.

Reach higher through the clouds and into the sky.

Close your eyes.

Reach even higher for five more seconds.

5…4…3…2…1.

Take a big breath in.

Breathe out and bring your arms down slowly.

Slowly open your eyes.

STRETCH

BEING A BUTTERFLY

Sit with your legs crossed.

Put your hands on your knees.

Sit up as tall as you can.

Can I see everyone sitting up tall?

We are going to practice being butterflies!

Let's crisscross our fingers and put them under our chins.

Our arms are our butterfly wings.

Let's practice moving our wings slowly up and down like we're flying.

Now, let's practice moving our wings up and down with our eyes closed.

Close your eyes and move your wings up and down.

Imagine you are flying through the blue and sunny sky.

Keep flying for 5 more seconds.

5…4…3…2…1.

Now, imagine you have landed on a pretty flower.

Breathe in the flower's beautiful smell.

Breathe out slowly.

Put your hands on your knees.

Slowly open your eyes.

STRETCH

REACH FOR YOUR TOES (SEATED)

Put your legs and feet together and straight out in front of you.

Put your hands on your legs.

Sit up as tall as you can.

Can I see everyone sitting up tall?

Now, we are going to reach our arms all the way up to the sky.

Wiggle your fingers.

Now, wiggle your toes in your shoes.

Slowly and carefully bend over and reach for your wiggling toes.

You can put your hands on your knees, or if you can reach them, you can touch your toes!

Now, close your eyes and keep reaching for your toes for 5 more seconds.

5…4…3…2…1.

Open your eyes and reach your arms all the way up to the sky again.

Wiggle your fingers.

Wiggle your toes in your shoes.

Slowly bring your arms down and put your hands on your legs.

Take a big breath in.

Breathe out slowly.

STRETCH

REACH FOR YOUR TOES (STANDING)

Stand with your legs and feet together and your arms by your sides.

Stand up as tall as you can.

Can I see everyone standing up tall?

Now, we are going to reach our arms all the way up to the sky.

Wiggle your fingers.

Now, wiggle your toes in your shoes.

Let's slowly and carefully bend over and reach for our wiggling toes.

You can put your hands on your knees, or if you can reach them, you can touch your toes!

Now, let's close our eyes and keep reaching for our toes for 5 more seconds.

5…4…3…2…1.

Open your eyes and reach your body and arms all the way up to the sky again.

Wiggle your fingers.

Wiggle your toes in your shoes.

Slowly bring your arms down by your sides.

Take a big breath in.

Breathe out slowly.

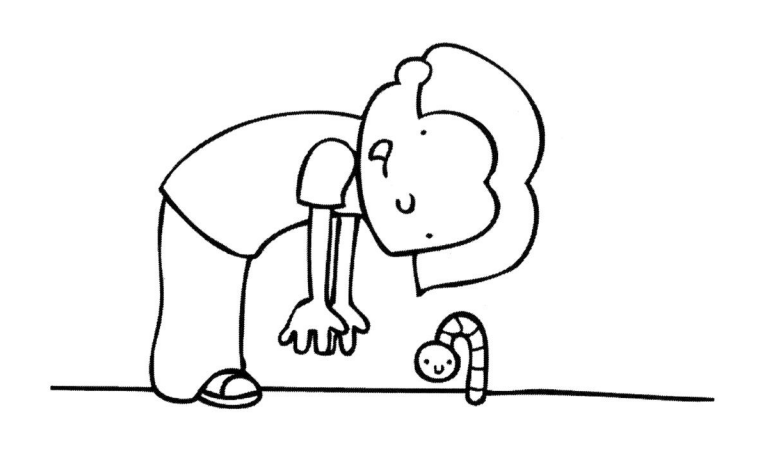

STAR STRETCH (STANDING)

Stand with your feet wide apart.

Stand up as tall as you can.

Can I see everyone standing up tall?

Stretch your arms and hands out to the sides like a star.

Spread your fingers wide.

Stretch even further and become an even bigger, brighter star.

Close your eyes.

Keep stretching for three more seconds.

3…2…1.

Bring your arms down slowly.

Breathe in.

Breathe out.

Slowly open your eyes.

STRETCH

STAR STRETCH (LYING DOWN)

Lie down on your back.

Get comfortable.

Stretch your arms and legs out to the sides like a star.

Spread your fingers wide.

Stretch even further and become an even bigger, brighter star.

Close your eyes.

Keep stretching for three more seconds.

3…2…1.

Relax your arms and legs.

Breathe in.

Breathe out.

Slowly open your eyes.

SEATED MOON

Sit with your legs crossed.

Put your hands on your knees.

Sit up as tall as you can.

Can I see everyone sitting up tall?

Reach your arms up to the sky.

Touch your fingertips together and make a full moon circle with your arms.

Look up at your beautiful moon circle.

Close your eyes.

Imagine what you might see in the nighttime sky.

[Wait 5 seconds]

Take a big breath in.

Breathe out and bring your arms down slowly.

Put your hands on your knees.

Slowly open your eyes.

STRETCH

STANDING MOON

Stand with your feet a little bit apart.

Stand up as tall as you can.

Can I see everyone standing up tall?

Reach your arms up to the sky.

Touch your fingertips together and make a full moon circle with your arms.

Look up at your bright moon circle.

Close your eyes.

Imagine what you might see in the nighttime sky.

[Wait 5 seconds]

Take a big breath in.

Breathe out and bring your arms down slowly.

Slowly open your eyes.

STRETCH

BEING A TREE

Stand with your feet a little bit apart.

Stand up as tall as you can.

Can I see everyone standing up tall?

Reach your arms straight up to the sky like tree branches.

Your fingers are your leaves.

Wiggle your leaves!

Lift up one foot and balance on one leg like a tree trunk.

Balance for 3 seconds.

3…2…1.

Put your foot back on the ground.

Bring your arms down slowly.

Take a big breath in.

Breath out slowly.

KINDERGARTEN

BREATHE

BIG HAPPY BREATH

We are going to practice big happy breath.

Sit with your legs crossed.

Get comfortable.

Place your hands on your knees.

Sit up tall so that your back is straight.

All the parts of your body are quiet and not moving.

Open your arms wide and take a big happy breath in through your nose.

Breathe out very slowly through your nose and give yourself a hug.

Open your arms wide and take a big happy breath in through your nose.

Breathe out very slowly through your nose and give yourself a hug.

Let's try one more big happy breath with our eyes closed.

Close your eyes.

Open your arms wide and take a big happy breath in through your nose.

Breathe out very slowly through your nose and give yourself a hug.

Place your hands on your knees.

Think about how you feel.

[Wait 5 seconds]

Slowly open your eyes.

SUN BREATHING

We are going to practice sun breathing.

Stand up tall with your arms by your sides.

Stand with your feet together.

All the parts of your body are quiet and not moving.

Imagine that you are the strong, bright, sparkling sun in the sky.

You are going to make the shape of the sun with your arms.

Take a big breath in and slowly bring your arms out to the sides and straight up over your head.

Touch the palms of your hands together.

Breathe out and slowly bring your arms down by your sides.

Close your eyes.

Now, breathe in, bring your arms up and imagine bringing all the sunshine into your body.

Breathe out, bring your arms down and imagine sending your sunshine out into the world.

Breathe in arms up.

Breathe out arms down.

Now, stand up tall with your arms by your sides.

Think about how you feel.

[Wait 5 seconds]

Slowy open your eyes

BREATHE

BUTTERFLY BREATHING

We are going to practice butterfly breathing.

Sit with the bottoms of your feet together with your knees out to the sides.

Rest your hands on your knees.

Sit up tall so that your back is straight.

All the parts of your body are quiet and not moving.

Think of your favorite color and imagine that you are a colorful butterfly.

Now, clasp your hands underneath your chin and lift your elbows out to the sides.

These are your colorful butterfly wings.

Slowly move your wings up and down and imagine you are a butterfly flying over your favorite outdoor place.

[Wait 5 seconds]

Now, take a big breath in through your nose and slowly lift your wings out and up.

Breathe out and slowly bring your wings down and together.

Close your eyes.

Breathe in and slowly lift your wings up.

Breathe out and slowly lower your wings down.

Breathe in and lift your wings up.

Breathe out and lower your wings down.

Rest your hands on your knees.

Think about how you feel.

[Wait 5 seconds]

Slowly open your eyes.

REACH FOR A STAR BREATH

We are going to practice reach for a star breath.

Stand up tall with your hands over your heart.

Stand with your feet together.

All the parts of your body are quiet and not moving.

Imagine the night sky filled with sparkling stars.

Slowly breathe in, reach one arm up into the night sky and take a star.

Slowly breathe out, bring your arm down and put the star in your heart.

Breathe in and reach the other arm up into the night sky and take another star.

Breathe out and put the star in your heart.

Breathe in and reach for a star.

Breathe out and put the star in your heart.

Put both hands on your heart.

Close your eyes.

Think about all of the stars you have in your heart.

[Wait 5 seconds]

Think about how you feel.

[Wait 5 seconds]

Slowly open your eyes.

BREATHE

TALL AND SMALL BREATHING

We are going to practice tall and small breathing.

Stand up tall with your arms by your sides.

Stand with your feet apart.

All the parts of your body are quiet and not moving.

Take a big breath in, reach your arms and fingers up and get tall.

Make fists, pull your elbows down, breathe out, and get small.

Breathe in, reach up and get tall.

Breathe out, bend down and get small.

Breathe in, reach up and get tall.

Breathe out, bend down and get small.

Breathe in, reach up and get tall.

Breathe out, bend down and get small.

Stand up tall with your arms by your sides.

Now, take a big breath in and breathe out slowly.

Close your eyes.

Think about how you feel.

[Wait 5 seconds]

Slowly open your eyes.

MAKE A WISH BREATH

We are going to practice make a wish breath.

Sit with your legs crossed.

Get comfortable.

Place your hands on your knees.

Sit up tall so that your back is straight.

All the parts of your body are quiet and not moving.

Imagine that you are going to make a wish as you blow out a magic candle.

Take a moment to think about your wish.

You are going to blow out the candle by taking one big breath in and blowing out three times.

Take a big breath in and blow out three times whoooo, whoooo, whoooo.

Now, close your eyes and make another wish.

Breathe in.

Blow out three times whoooo, whoooo, whoooo.

One more time.

Breathe in.

Blow out three times whoooo, whoooo, whoooo.

Think about how you feel.

[Wait 5 seconds]

Slowly open your eyes.

FOCUS

FOCUS

LISTENING TO THE BELL

We are going to practice listening to the bell.

Sit with your legs crossed.

Get comfortable.

Place your hands on your knees.

Sit up tall so that your back is straight.

Close your eyes.

All the parts of your body are quiet and not moving.

Try not to move your fingers or toes.

The bell will sound loud at first, then it will become softer, then it will stop ringing.

Pay attention to the sound of the bell until it stops ringing.

When the bell stops ringing, listen to the quiet.

[Ring bell three times in a row, then wait for the bell to stop ringing]

Now, gently wiggle your fingers.

Gently wiggle your toes.

Take a big breath in and breathe out slowly.

Think about how you feel.

[Wait 5 seconds]

Slowly open your eyes.

SITTING PEACEFULLY

We are going to practice sitting peacefully.

Sit with your legs crossed.

Get comfortable.

Place your hands on your knees.

Sit up tall so that your back is straight.

Sitting peacefully means your whole body is quiet and not moving.

Close your eyes

Your eyes are quiet and peaceful.

Your head is quiet and peaceful.

Your shoulders are quiet and peaceful.

Your belly is quiet and peaceful.

Your knees are quiet and peaceful.

Your feet are quiet and peaceful.

Your whole body is quiet and peaceful.

[Wait 5 seconds]

Breathe in slowly.

Breathe out slowly.

Now, gently wiggle your fingers.

Gently wiggle your toes in your shoes.

Take a big breath in and breathe out slowly.

Think about how you feel.

[Wait 5 seconds]

Slowly open your eyes.

FOCUS

"I AM CALM"

We are going to practice "I Am Calm."

Sit with your legs crossed.

Get comfortable.

Place your hands on your knees.

Sit up tall so that your back is straight.

All the parts of your body are quiet and not moving.

Let's say the words, "I am calm" quietly together three times.

"I am calm."

"I am calm."

"I am calm."

Now, breathe in and think about the words "I am."

Breathe out and think about the word "calm."

Breathe in and think about the words "I am."

Breathe out and think about the word "calm."

Now, let's try this with our eyes closed.

Breathe in, "I am."

Breathe out, "calm."

Breathe in, "I am."

Breathe out, "calm."

Now, take a big breath in and breathe out slowly.

Think about how you feel.

[Wait 5 seconds]

Slowly open your eyes.

FOCUS

MUSIC SCRIBBLE

We are going to practice music scribble.

Sit up tall so that your back is straight.

Place your pencil or crayon on the piece of paper in front of you.

You are going to scribble on your piece of paper any way you want to, as you listen to the music.

If the music is fast, you can scribble fast.

If the music is slow, you can scribble slowly.

It doesn't matter how anyone else scribbles, just have fun doing it your own way.

Now, listen very closely to the music and feel the music as you begin to scribble.

[Music]

Now, close your eyes.

Pay attention to the feeling of your hand scribbling on the paper.

Keep scribbling.

[Music ends]

Keep your eyes closed.

Put your pencil or crayon down.

Rest your hands in your lap.

Now, take a big breath in and breathe out slowly.

Think about how you feel.

[Wait 5 seconds]

Slowly open your eyes.

FOCUS

LOOKING AT ONE THING

We are going to practice looking at one thing. [Students sit in a circle. Leader chooses the object and places it in the center of the circle.]

Sit with your legs crossed.

Get comfortable.

Place your hands on your knees.

Sit up tall so that your back is straight.

All the parts of your body are quiet and not moving.

Look at the object in the middle of the circle.

Notice what color it is.

Notice what shape it is.

Notice if it is big or little.

Let your eyes relax while you look at the object.

If your eyes look away, bring them back to the object.

Try to keep your body perfectly still.

[Wait for students to look at the object for 10 seconds.]

Now, close your eyes and let your eyes rest.

[Wait 5 seconds]

Take a big breath in and breathe out slowly.

Think about how you feel.

[Wait 5 seconds]

Slowly open your eyes.

FOCUS

LISTENING TO COUNTING

We are going to practice listening to counting. [Create longer periods of silence in between each number as you count down]

Sit with your legs crossed.

Get comfortable.

Place your hands on your knees.

Sit up tall so that your back is straight.

All the parts of your body are quiet and not moving.

Close your eyes.

Listen to my voice as I slowly count down from 5 to 1.

Listen to the sound of my voice and the quiet in between the numbers.

5 *[Wait 2 seconds]*

4 *[Wait 4 seconds]*

3 *[Wait 6 seconds]*

2 *[Wait 8 seconds]*

1 *[Wait 10 seconds]*

Keep your eyes closed.

Now, take a big breath in and breathe out slowly.

Think about how you feel.

[Wait 5 seconds]

Slowly open your eyes.

FOCUS

ENERGY HANDS

We are going to practice energy hands.

Sit with your legs crossed.

Get comfortable.

Place your hands on your knees.

Sit up tall so that your back is straight.

All the parts of your body are quiet and not moving.

Bring your hands together.

Rub them together.

Rub your hands together faster.

Keep rubbing.

Now, clap your hands.

Keep clapping.

Clap as fast as you can.

Clap for yourself.

Clap for everyone in the room.

Now, rub your hands together again.

Feel your hands getting warmer and warmer.

Listen to the sound of your hands rubbing together.

FREEZE!

Imagine that you are holding a basketball with both of your hands facing each other.

Close your eyes.

ENERGY HANDS (cont.)

Without touching your hands together, move both hands towards each other.

Feel the tingling and warmth in between your hands.

Slowly move your hands toward each other and apart without touching them together.

[Wait 10 seconds]

Now, move your hands together until they touch.

Rest your hands on your knees.

Now, take a big breath in and breathe out slowly.

Think about how you feel.

[Wait 5 seconds]

Slowly open your eyes.

FOCUS

BEE'S BUZZ

We are going to practice bee's buzz.

Sit with your legs crossed.

Get comfortable.

Place your hands on your knees.

Sit up tall so that your back is straight.

All the parts of your body are quiet and not moving.

When bees buzz, they make a quiet humming sound.

A quiet humming sound sounds like this: hmmmmmmmm.

Let's all try making a quiet humming sound.

Take a big breath in.

Breathe out and quietly hum: hmmmmmmmm.

Let's try that again.

Take a big breath in.

Breathe out and quietly hum: hmmmmmmmm:

Now, let's try it again with our eyes closed and our ears covered.

Close your eyes and cover your ears.

Take a big breath in.

Breathe out and quietly hum: hmmmmmmmm.

Rest your hands on your knees.

Think about how you feel.

[Wait 5 seconds]

Slowly open your eyes.

RELAX

RELAX

PLEASE RELAX

We are going to practice "please relax."

We are going to relax each part of our body.

Lie on your back with your legs straight and your arms by your sides.

All the parts of your body are quiet and not moving.

Close your eyes.

Breathe in slowly.

Breathe out slowly.

Place both hands on your head.

Quietly whisper, "head please relax."

Place both hands on your shoulders.

Quietly whisper, "shoulders please relax."

Place both hands on your belly.

Feel your belly move gently up and down as you breathe in and out.

Quietly whisper, "belly please relax."

Place both hands on your legs.

Quietly whisper, "legs please relax."

Now, relax your arms by your sides.

Slowly wiggle your fingers.

Stop moving your fingers.

Quietly whisper, "fingers please relax."

Slowly wiggle your toes in your shoes.

Stop moving your toes.

PLEASE RELAX (cont.)

Quietly whisper, "toes please relax."

Your whole body feels relaxed.

Rest here for a moment.

[Wait 10 seconds]

Now, bend both knees.

Give them a hug.

Come up to a seated position with your legs crossed.

Keep your eyes closed.

Put your hands on your knees.

Now, take a big breath in and breathe out slowly.

Think about how you feel.

[Wait 5 seconds]

Slowly open your eyes.

PLEASE RELAX - SEATED

We are going to practice "please relax."

We are going to relax each part of our body.

Sit up tall so that your back is straight.

All the parts of your body are quiet and not moving.

Close your eyes.

Breathe in slowly.

Breathe out slowly.

Place both hands on your head.

Quietly whisper, "head please relax."

Place both hands on your shoulders.

Quietly whisper, "shoulders please relax."

Place both hands on your belly.

Feel your belly move gently up and down as you breathe in and out.

Quietly whisper, "belly please relax."

Place both hands on your legs.

Quietly whisper, "legs please relax."

Now, relax your hands on your lap.

Slowly wiggle your fingers.

Stop moving your fingers.

Quietly whisper, "fingers please relax."

Slowly wiggle your toes in your shoes.

Stop moving your toes.

Quietly whisper, "toes please relax."

PLEASE RELAX - SEATED (cont.)

Your whole body feels relaxed.

Rest here for a moment.

[Wait 10 seconds]

Keep your eyes closed and stay still.

Notice your breathing.

Notice the quiet.

Now, take a big breath in and breathe out slowly.

Think about how you feel.

[Wait 5 seconds]

Slowly open your eyes.

RELAX

SHAKE LIKE SPAGHETTI

We are going to practice "shake like spaghetti."

Stand up tall with your arms by your sides.

Stand with your feet apart.

All the parts of your body are quiet and not moving.

Imagine that your entire body is made out of spaghetti noodles.

Now, gently shake one spaghetti arm.

Shake it up high.

Shake it down low.

Now, shake both spaghetti arms.

Shake them to one side.

Shake them to the other side.

Now, close your eyes and shake, shake, shake your spaghetti arms.

Shake your spaghetti arms as fast as you can.

Now open your eyes, keep shaking your spaghetti arms and shake one spaghetti leg.

Shake the other spaghetti leg.

Close your eyes and shake your whole spaghetti body.

Shake faster.

Keep shaking.

FREEZE!

Keep your eyes closed and stand very still.

Feel the tingling in your arms and legs.

Listen to the quiet.

Now, take a big breath in and breathe out slowly.

Think about how you feel.

[Wait 5 seconds]

Slowly open your eyes.

RELAX

COVERING YOUR EYES

We are going to practice covering your eyes.

Sit with your legs crossed.

Get comfortable.

Place your hands on your knees

Sit up tall so that your back is straight.

All the parts of your body are quiet and not moving.

Bring your hands together.

Rub them together.

Rub your hands together faster!

Keep rubbing.

Listen to the sound of your hands rubbing together.

Feel your hands getting warmer and warmer.

Now, stop rubbing.

Close your eyes.

Gently put your warm hands over your eyes with your fingers on your forehead.

Cover your eyes so that no light comes in.

Let your eyes rest.

[Wait 10 seconds]

Rest your hands on your knees.

Now, take a big breath in and breathe out slowly.

Think about how you feel.

[Wait 5 seconds]

Slowly open your eyes.

STRETCH

STRETCH

SEATED MOUNTAIN

We are going to practice seated mountain.

Sit with your legs crossed.

Get comfortable.

Place your hands on your knees.

Sit up tall so that your back is straight.

Imagine that you are a tall mountain.

Mountains do not make any sounds and do not move.

A mountain is connected to the Earth and reaches all the way up into the sky.

Your legs are the bottom part of the mountain, connecting to the Earth.

From your waist to the top of your head is the top part of the mountain.

Now, reach your arms all the way up to the sky through the clouds.

Close your eyes.

Imagine what you might see from the top of your tall mountain.

You might see the sun, birds flying by, an airplane or a rainbow.

[Wait 10 seconds]

Now, slowly lower your arms down and rest your hands on your knees.

Take a big breath in and breathe out slowly.

Think about how you feel.

[Wait 5 seconds]

Slowly open your eyes.

STRETCH

STANDING MOUNTAIN

We are going to practice standing mountain.

Stand up tall with your arms by your sides.

Stand with your feet together.

All the parts of your body are quiet and not moving.

Imagine that you are a tall mountain.

Mountains do not make any sounds and do not move.

A mountain is connected to the Earth and reaches all the way up into the sky.

Your legs and feet are the bottom part of the mountain, connecting to the Earth.

From your waist to the top of your head is the top part of the mountain.

Now, reach your arms all the way up to the sky through the clouds.

Close your eyes.

Imagine what you might see from the top of your tall mountain.

You might see the sun, birds flying by, an airplane or a rainbow.

[Wait 10 seconds]

Now, slowly lower your arms down and rest your hands by your sides.

Take a big breath in and breathe out slowly.

Think about how you feel.

[Wait 5 seconds]

Slowly open your eyes.

STRETCH

SEATED HALF MOON

We are going to practice seated half moon.

Sit with your legs crossed.

Get comfortable.

Place your hands on your knees.

Sit up tall so that your back is straight.

All the parts of your body are quiet and not moving.

You are going to make the shape of a half moon with your body.

Stretch your arms straight up over your head and reach for the stars.

Lower one arm down and place your hand on the floor next to you.

Bend to the side, making a half moon shape with your body.

Close your eyes and imagine your body is the bright moon in the night sky.

Breathe in and get bigger.

Breathe out and get brighter.

Imagine all the stars sparkling around you.

Open your eyes, stretch both arms straight up over your head and reach for the stars.

Lower the other arm down and place your hand on the floor next to you.

Bend to the other side, making a half moon shape with your body.

Close your eyes.

Breathe in and get bigger.

Breathe out and get brighter.

Imagine all of the colorful planets around you.

Keep your eyes closed and stretch both arms straight up over your head.

Slowly lower your arms and rest your hands on your knees.

Now, take a big breath in and breathe out slowly.

Think about how you feel. *[Wait 5 seconds]*

Slowly open your eyes.

STRETCH

STANDING HALF MOON

We are going to practice standing half moon.

Stand up tall with your arms by your sides.

Stand with your feet together.

All the parts of your body are quiet and not moving.

You are going to make the shape of a half moon with your body.

Stretch your arms straight up over your head and reach for the stars.

Bend to one side, making a half moon shape with your body.

Close your eyes and imagine your body is the bright moon in the night sky.

Breathe in and get bigger.

Breathe out and get brighter.

Imagine all the stars sparkling around you.

Open your eyes, stretch your arms straight up over your head and reach for the stars.

Bend to the other side, making a half moon shape with your body.

Close your eyes.

Breathe in and get bigger.

Breathe out and get brighter.

Imagine all of the colorful planets around you.

Keep your eyes closed and stretch both arms straight up over your head.

Slowly lower your arms and rest your hands by your sides.

Now, take a big breath in and breathe out slowly.

Think about how you feel. *[Wait 5 seconds]*

Slowly open your eyes.

STRETCH

TWIST AND COUNT

We are going to practice twist and count.

Sit with your legs crossed.

Get comfortable.

Place your hands on your knees.

Sit up tall so that your back is straight.

All the parts of your body are quiet and not moving.

Place one hand on the floor behind you and move the other hand across your body and put it on your knee.

Take a big breath in and sit up tall.

Slowly breathe out and gently twist toward the hand behind you.

Look over your shoulder.

Stay in your twist and close your eyes.

We will stay in our twist for three counts.

Let's count quietly together.

1.....2.....3.

Open your eyes and come back to the center.

Place your hands on your knees.

Sit up tall.

Place the other hand on the floor behind you and reach the opposite hand across your body and rest it on your knee.

Take a big breath in and sit up tall.

Slowly breathe out and gently twist toward the hand behind you.

Look over your shoulder.

Stay in your twist and close your eyes.

TWIST AND COUNT (cont.)

We will stay in our twist for three counts.

Let's count quietly together.

1.....2.....3.

Keep your eyes closed and come back to the center.

Place your hands on your knees.

Now, take a big breath in and breathe out slowly.

Think about how you feel.

[Wait 5 seconds]

Slowly open your eyes.

STRETCH

REACH FOR YOUR TOES - SEATED

We are going to practice reaching for your toes.

Sit with your legs straight out in front of you.

Your toes and knees are pointing up.

Sit up tall so that your back is straight.

Get comfortable.

Place your hands by your sides.

Reach your arms straight up over your head.

Wiggle your fingers.

Wiggle your toes in your shoes.

Slowly and carefully bend over and reach for your toes.

You can put your hands on your knees, ankles, or feet.

Now, close your eyes and keep reaching for your toes.

[Wait 10 seconds]

Sit up tall and reach your arms straight up over your head.

Wiggle your fingers.

Wiggle your toes.

Slowly lower your arms and rest your hands by your sides.

Now, take a big breath in and breathe out slowly.

Think about how you feel.

[Wait 5 seconds]

Slowly open your eyes.

REACH FOR YOUR TOES - STANDING

We are going to practice reaching for your toes.

Stand up tall with your arms by your sides.

Stand with your feet together.

All the parts of your body are quiet and not moving.

Reach your arms straight up over your head.

Wiggle your fingers.

Wiggle your toes in your shoes.

Slowly and carefully bend over and reach for your toes.

You can put your hands on your knees, ankles, or feet.

Now, close your eyes and keep reaching for your toes.

Relax your head and neck.

[Wait 10 seconds]

Stand up tall and reach your arms straight up over your head.

Wiggle your fingers.

Wiggle your toes.

Slowly lower your arms by your sides.

Now, take a big breath in and breathe out slowly.

Think about how you feel.

[Wait 5 seconds]

Slowly open your eyes.